SUSAN BAYLISS

Turbo Pascal

A Quick Program Reference Guide

For IBM®PC/XT/AT and compatibles

H. J. Bomanns

An Abacus Data-Becker Book

First Printing, August 1987
Printed in U.S.A.

ISBN   1-55755-001-8

Contents

Introduction

This Turbo Pascal Program Reference Guide is not intended to be an introduction to the Pascal programming language. Rather, it is designed to be a quick reference tool for the intermediate to advanced level Turbo programmer. We assume that you have a general knowledge of Pascal and some experience working with an IBM PC or compatible, or a CP/M-80/86 computer.

About Turbo Pascal

Except for GW-BASIC and BASICA from Microsoft, Borland's Turbo Pascal is probably the most widely-used programming language on the IBM PCs. There are many advantages to programming in the Pascal language instead of BASIC. Turbo Pascal programs run considerably faster than BASIC programs, and the source programs are more manageable because of the structure of the Pascal language. In addition, extensions to Turbo Pascal have made it even easier to adapt programs to use any of the hardware-specific features of the PC, such as graphics, specialized printers and other input and output devices. This means that you'll be able to squeeze every last bit of power out of your PC.

About this guide

When you work with Turbo Pascal on a regular basis, you often need to know the syntax, name, or parameters of a Turbo Pascal function or procedure in a hurry. Because this Program Reference Guide lists all the Turbo Pascal commands in alphabetical order, you can keep it right next to your PC and quickly look up any

1

command without having to consult a bulky 3-ring user manual or reference book.

This guide describes program command syntax using the familiar characters and placeholders commonly used to describe MS-DOS command syntax:

Abc   Parameter names are upper- and lower-case letters printed as italic text. This lets you distinguish between parameters and commands more easily.

[ ]   Parameters enclosed in square brackets are optional. These parameters are not necessary for the execution of the command. They usually control special functions of the command.

| The vertical bar separates alternative parameters. Only <u>one</u> of the parameters in a list separated by this character can be used.

ResWd All reserved words and standard identifiers appear in boldface type.

`Prg.code`

      Samples of program code are printed in smaller typewriter-style text.

(x)   The boldface letter or groups of letters in parentheses at the right of each "box" indicates whether the word is a function (**F**), standard function (**SF**), statement (**S**), procedure (**P**), standard procedure (**SP**), array (**A**) or operator (**O**).

Using the Indexes

If you know the name of a keyword, but are unsure of its usage or syntax, refer to the *QuickIndex* at the back of the book. Each Turbo Pascal command is listed there in alphabetical order, and refers you to the page number(s) where that keyword can be found in the guide.

If you are looking for a keyword to perform a specific task, but are unsure of its name or syntax, refer to the **Subject Index**. There you'll find a list of keywords grouped according to usage, along with short descriptions of their effects, and references to relevant page numbers.

For information and references to general Turbo Pascal information and specific operations, refer to the last **Index** of the guide.

Here's a quick explanation of the format this guide uses to describe Turbo Pascal's commands, statements and functions, and their parameters:

Keyword   **Brief description   (Type)**

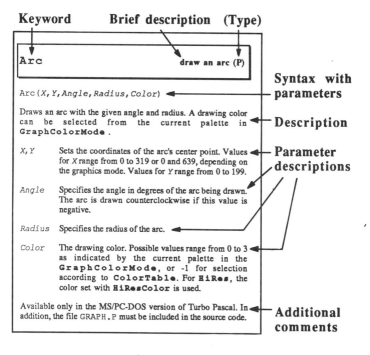

```
Arc                              draw an arc (P)
```

Syntax with parameters

`Arc(X,Y,Angle,Radius,Color)`

Draws an arc with the given angle and radius. A drawing color can be selected from the current palette in `GraphColorMode` .

Description

`X,Y`   Sets the coordinates of the arc's center point. Values for X range from 0 to 319 or 0 and 639, depending on the graphics mode. Values for Y range from 0 to 199.

Parameter descriptions

`Angle`   Specifies the angle in degrees of the arc being drawn. The arc is drawn counterclockwise if this value is negative.

`Radius`   Specifies the radius of the arc.

`Color`   The drawing color. Possible values range from 0 to 3 as indicated by the current palette in the `GraphColorMode`, or -1 for selection according to `ColorTable`. For `HiRes`, the color set with `HiResColor` is used.

Available only in the MS/PC-DOS version of Turbo Pascal. In addition, the file GRAPH.P must be included in the source code.

Additional comments

General Information

Installing Turbo Pascal

Before you can use Turbo Pascal, you must first install it on
your PC. This installation tells Turbo what monitor you are
using, what key combinations are used in the editor, and where
the error messages can be found on the disk. Only the major
points of the installation process will be described here. You can
find complete information in several chapters of the Turbo
Pascal Reference Manual.

The Turbo Pascal disk has an installation program named
`TINST.COM` and a related file named `TINST.MSG`. When you
call the program `TINST`, you can specify the screen, key
assignment in the editor, and search path for the error message
file.

[S]creen installation

The easiest installation contains the version intended for an IBM
PC or compatible. The only decision you have to make is the
type of monitor you are working with, and whether you want 40
or 80 columns per line. You can also synchronize the output to
suppress the screen flickering on a color monitor.

For other versions you will get a list of various terminals from
which you can choose yours or one similar to it. For more
uncommon terminals you can make your own definitions by
answering a set of questions about the terminal. Details can be
found in the Turbo Pascal Reference Manual starting at page 12
and in Appendix L.

[C]ommand installation

All of the functions for manipulating the program text are
performed with various key combinations. Borland designed the
editor to use many of the key combinations found in MicroPro's
WordStar© word processor. You can adapt the key combinations
to your own tastes with this installation option. For example, if
you don't like the combination Ctrl+K+Y for deleting a block,
you can easily change it to Ctrl+B+D, for example.

Details can be found in Appendix L of the Turbo Pascal
Reference Manual.

[M]sg file path

When Turbo is compiling a program, it outputs a message when
it finds an error. This message can be in English, or it can be
just an error number. The error messages are stored in the file
TURBO.MSG. Here you can specify where on the disk this file
can be found. Generally this file is placed in a RAM disk in
order to display the messages on the screen as quickly as
possible. The search path is then:

```
D:\TURBO.MSG
```

Starting Turbo Pascal

```
Turbo                                    start Turbo Pascal
```

After you've successfully installed the program, you can begin working with Turbo Pascal. Simply type:

```
Turbo
```

and press Enter to load the Turbo Pascal compiler/editor.

Depending on the version, a display similar to the following appears:

```
---------------------------------------
Turbo Pascal System        Version3.01A
                                  PC-DOS
Copyright (C) 1983,84,85 Borland INC.
---------------------------------------
Color Display 80x25
Include error messages (Y/N)?
```

If you type Y in response to the prompt "Include error messages (Y/N)?", complete error messages are displayed. Otherwise, only error numbers are displayed. The file TURBO.MSG takes up about 1.5K of memory. Turbo's easy-to-understand error messages make it worth using up this memory.

Turbo Pascal displays a menu similar to the following (again, depending on the version):

```
            Logged drive: C
            Active directory: \Turbo
            Work file:
            Main file:
            Edit      Compile  Run    Save
            Dir       Quit  compiler Options
            Text:      0 bytes
            Free: 62024 bytes
```

6

You select individual options by pressing the first (capitalized) letter of the option, displayed in high intensity in the menu:

Logged drive

>   Specify the drive that is used for subsequent disk access. All programs are saved or loaded from this drive.

Active directory

>   Specify the subdirectory to which the subsequent load and save operations are directed.

Work file

>   Specify the name of the source program that you want to edit or create.

Main file

>   If you use include files, specify the name of the source program that contains the include files.

Edit   Specify that you will enter the Turbo Pascal editor after loading or executing a Turbo program.

Compile

>   Starts compiling the source program. Depending on the settings in the compiler Options menu, the object code is written to memory, or to a file in the specified subdirectory on the specified drive with a .COM or .CHN extension.

Run   If the Memory option is selected in the compiler Options menu, the source program is compiled to memory and then executed.

Save   Saves the program being edited to the specified subdirectory in the specified drive.

Dir   Displays the directory in DOS format DIR /W. A different drive/directory and a mask with the wildcards * and ? can be specified.

7

Quit   Ends the Turbo Pascal session. If the source program
            was changed and has not been saved after the change,
            you're asked if you want to save it.

Text: xxxxx bytes
Free: xxxxx bytes
            Indicates how many bytes the source program
            occupies (Text), and how many bytes are still
            available for the editor (Free).

compiler Options
            Specify the important options for the compilation
            process. The following menu appears:

compile- Memory
         Com-file
         cHn-file
         command line Parameters:
         Find run-time error Quit

         Memory
         The source program is compiled directly into
         memory and can be executed with Run from the
         Main Menu.

         Com-file
         The source program is compiled and stored on the
         specified drive and subdirectory as a .COM file.

         cHn-file
         The source program is compiled and stored on the
         given drive and subdirectory as a .CHN file. This is a
         file that does not contain a run-time module, is called
         from another Turbo Pascal program (.COM), and uses
         the run-time module of the calling program. Here
         you can also make specifications relating to the
         program and data memory size (see Chain and
         Execute).

         command line Parameters:
         Some Turbo commands let you specify parameters or
         options on the command line. The values are stored

in the standard functions **ParamStr** and **ParamCount**. When compiling in the Memory mode, the parameters to be passed are specified here.

Find run-time error
In some cases, a Turbo Pascal program can terminate with the error message:

```
Run-time error xx, PC=yyyy
Program aborted
```

xx indicates the error number and yyyy indicates the current value of the program counter. Write down both numbers. Then start Turbo, load the source program and select this menu option. You are then asked to enter the program counter state yyyy. Turbo Pascal shows the point where the error occurred. This allows you to find and correct run-time errors easily.

Quit   Returns you to the Main Menu.

Constants, Types, and Variables

Turbo Pascal supports the following standard scalar types:

BYTE   Integer (0 to 255). Requires 1 byte of memory.

INTEGER
            Integer (-32768 to +32767). Requires 2 bytes of memory.

REAL   Floating-point with a range from 1E-38 to 1E+38. Requires 6 bytes of memory.

BOOLEAN
            Value of True or False. Requires 1 byte of memory.

CHAR   Integer with value range according to ASCII codes from 0 to 255. Requires 1 byte of memory.

9

STRING   An ARRAY of CHAR, integers with a value range
          from 0 to 255 according to ASCII codes. Memory
          requirements range from 0 to 255 bytes for the
          string length plus one byte beyond the string length.

Expressions that correspond to the supported data types can be
used as constants. User-defined data types can be defined with
type and then declared with **var**. This can involve simple
variables, records, arrays, or sets.

Key Assignments in the Editor

In Turbo Pascal, all editor functions are performed using key
combinations. These combinations are almost identical to those
used by the WordStar© word processing program from
MicroPro. Borland chose this method because is a very popular
editor for CP/M and MS-DOS computers. These key
assignments can be changed to suit your preferences. The
standard assignments are listed below. Details can be found in
the Turbo Pascal Reference Manual starting on page 19.

Cursor control and movement

Moves the cursor one line up.	**Ctrl+E** or **Cursor up**
Moves the cursor one line down.	**Ctrl+X** or **Cursor down**
Moves the cursor one column to the left.	**Ctrl+S** or **Cursor left**
Moves the cursor one column to the right.	**Ctrl+D** or **Cursor right**
Moves one page back.	**Ctrl+R** or **PgUp**
Moves one page forward.	**Ctrl+C** or **PgDn**

Moves the cursor to the start of the word to the left of the cursor.	**Ctrl+A or Ctrl+Cursor left**
Moves the cursor to the start of the word to the right of the cursor.	**Ctrl+F or Ctrl+Cursor right**
Scrolls the listing up line by line.	**Ctrl+W**
Scrolls the listing down line by line.	**Ctrl+Z**
Sets the cursor to the top of the screen.	**Ctrl+Q+E or Home**
Sets the cursor to the bottom of the screen.	**Ctrl+Q+X or End**
Sets the cursor to the start of the file (first line).	**Ctrl+Q+R or Ctrl+PgUp**
Sets the cursor to the end of the file (last line).	**Ctrl+Q+C or Ctrl+PgDn**
Places the cursor in the first column of the current line.	**Ctrl+Q+S or Ctrl+Home**
Places the cursor behind the last character on the current line.	**Ctrl+Q+D or Ctrl+End**
Places the cursor at the start of a marked block.	**Ctrl+Q+B**
Places the cursor at the end of a marked block.	**Ctrl+Q+K**
Moves the cursor to its location before current input was made.	**Ctrl+Q+P**
Moves the cursor to the first character of the word directly above the cursor in the previous line.	**Ctrl+I or Tab**
Enables or disables automatic indentation.	**Ctrl+Q+I**

Miscellaneous functions

Exits the editor and jumps to the main menu.	**Ctrl+K+D**
Allows characters with ASCII values less than 32 (=space) to be entered in the text.	**Ctrl+P**
Terminates a command or input.	**Ctrl+U**

Inserting and deleting

Switches from Insert mode to Overwrite mode and back again.	**Ctrl+V** **or Ins**
Deletes the character at the current cursor location. The characters to the right of the cursor are moved to the left.	**Ctrl+G** **or Del**
Deletes the character to the left of the cursor. The rest of the line is moved to the left.	**Ctrl+H or** **Backspace**
Deletes the line that the cursor is located. The lines following it are moved up.	**Ctrl+Y**
Inserts a line break. The lines below are moved down.	**Ctrl+N** **or Enter**
Deletes the rest of the line from the cursor position on.	**Ctrl+Q+Y**
Restores the text previously changed, if the cursor was not moved out of the line immediately after the change.	**Ctrl+Q+L**

Block functions

Marks the start of a block.	**Ctrl+K+B**
Marks the end of a block. The marked block is displayed in a different color than the rest of the text.	**Ctrl+K+K**
Marks the word that the cursor is located on as a block.	**Ctrl+K+T**
Makes a marked block visible or invisible. Before additional block operations can be performed the block must be visible.	**Ctrl+K+H**
Copies a marked block beginning at the current cursor position. The marking of the block is placed at the new position, and the original marked block returns to normal video.	**Ctrl+K+C**
Moves a marked block from its original position to behind the cursor position. The marking of the block remains at its new position.	**Ctrl+K+V**
Deletes a marked block.	**Ctrl+K+Y**
Writes a marked block to disk. A prompt for the filename will appear in the first line of the screen.	**Ctrl+K+W**
Reads in a text from disk, and treats the text as a block. A prompt for the filename will appear in the first line of the screen. The read file is inserted at the current cursor location.	**Ctrl+K+R**

Search operations

Searches for a string within a program. A prompt for the string will appear in the first line of the screen. The following options can be specified for the search procedure:	**Ctrl+Q+F**
Search backwards, toward the start of the file	B
Search the entire file	G
Search for the *n*th occurrence in the file	*n*
No difference between upper- and lower-case	U
Search for whole words only	W

Options can be combined.

Replace operations

Searches for a string with a program and replaces it with another string. The following options can be specified for search/replace:	**Ctrl+Q+A**
Search/replace backwards, toward the start of the file	B
Search/replace in the entire file	G
Search/replace the next *n*th occurrences in the file	*n*
Replace all occurrences without asking	N
No difference between upper and lower-case	U
Search for whole words only	W
Repeat the last search or search/replace operation	**Ctrl+L**

Options can be combined.

Compiler Directives

Compiler directives can be imbedded in the source program. These options are enclosed inside braces { }. The syntax for a compiler directive is the character $ followed by a single letter; then + (enable), − (disable), or a number. Turbo recognizes these directives and changes the method of compilation as requested. Multiple directives can be specified, separated by commas. For more details see the Turbo Pascal Reference Manual, page 313.

{ $B+/- }   default: { $B+ }

Sets the input/output device for execution (not compilation).

+   CON:

-         TRM:

This directive is in effect during the entire program and cannot be changed.

{ $C+/- }   default: { $C+ }

Controls the functions of the key combinations Ctrl+S and Ctrl+C during execution (not compilation).

+   The user can press Ctrl+C to terminate a program
             following **Read** or **ReadLn**; the user can press
             Ctrl+S to turn screen output off and on.

-            The Ctrl+C and Ctrl+S keys are disabled.

This option is in effect during the entire program and cannot be
changed.

{ $I+/- }   default: **{ $I+ }**

Controls Turbo Pascal error handling during execution (not
compilation).

+   Turbo handles errors.

-            Error handling is done within the program by testing
             IOresult.

This option can be turned on and off as desired within the
program.

{ $R+/- }   default: **{ $R- }**

Controls run-time testing of array bounds.

+   Checks indices to ensure they are within the limits
             specified at the declaration of the array.

-            Indices are not tested. Variables or program segments
             may be overwritten if array bounds are exceeded.

This option can be turned on and off as desired within the
program.

{ $U+/- }   default: { $U- }

Controls the termination of the program by the user.

+   Terminates the program when Ctrl+C is pressed.

-          The program can only be terminated with **halt**.

This option can be turned on and off as desired within the program.

{ $V+/- }   default: { $V+ }

Controls checking of parameter variable types.

+   Variable types passed to a procedure or function are checked.

-          No variable type checking.

This option can be turned on and off as desired within the program.

MS-DOS Compiler Directives

{ $D+/- }   default: { $D+ }

Controls text file status checking.

+   MS-DOS is asked for the status of a text file opened by **Append**, **Reset** or **Rewrite**. Buffers are disabled if the file is a device.

–   All input and output operations are performed via
         buffer.

This option can be turned on or off as desired within the
program.

{ $Fn }   default: { $F16 }

Specifies the number of files that can be open at one time.

n   The number of files open at one time. Values can
          range from 0 to 16.

This option is in effect during the entire program and cannot be
changed.

{ $Gn }   default: { $G0 }

Controls the definition of the standard input file buffer.

n   Specifies the input buffer size. The default ($G0) is
          CON: or TRM:. Any other number calls the
          appropriate MS-DOS input handle.

This option is in effect during the entire program and cannot be
changed.

{ $Pn }   default: { $P0 }

Controls the definition of the standard output file buffer.

n   Specifies the output buffer size. The default ($P0) is
             CON: or TRM:. Any other number calls the
             appropriate MS-DOS output handle.

This option is in effect during the entire program and cannot be
changed.

16-bit Compiler Directives

{ $K+/- }	default: { $K+ }

Controls stack checking code generation.

+   Preceding each subprogram call, the stack is checked
             to ensure sufficient memory for local variables.

−   The stack capacity is not checked.

This option can be turned on and off as desired within the
program.

CP/M-80 Compiler Directives

{ $A+/- }	default: { $A+ }

Controls absolute code generation.

+   Absolute (non-recursive) code is generated by the
             compiler.

−   Recursive code is generated by the compiler.

This option is in effect during the entire program and cannot be changed.

{ $Wn }   default: { $W2 }

Specifies the degree of nesting allowed for **with** statements.

n   The number of **with...do** loops allowed within a
               program block. Values range from 1 to 9.

This option is in effect during the entire program and cannot be changed.

{ $X+/- }   default: { $X+ }

Controls optimization of arrays during compilation.

+   Arrays are optimized for maximum execution speed.

–   Compiled code size is minimized.

This option is in effect during the entire program and cannot be changed.

Include Files

Another compiler option allows program sections to be loaded
from the disk during compilation. This allows programs larger
than available memory to be compiled. This also allows
programs to be written in modules:

{$I *Filespec*}	**Include files**

The file specified by *Filespec* is inserted into the program
source code and compiled.

Filespec

> The drive, path, and name of the file to be loaded.
> The drive and path only need to be specified if they
> differ from those defined in the main menu.

Turbo Pascal Commands

+, -, /, *   basic calculations (O)

```
Result = Expression_1 + Expression_2
Result = Expression_1 - Expression_2
Result = Expression_1 / Expression_2
Result = Expression_1 * Expression_2
```

Basic arithmetic operations are performed using the characters +, -, /, and *.

Expression
> Can be a constant, a variable of type INTEGER, BYTE, or REAL, or the result of mathematical functions. As many expressions as desired can be specified. Operators can also be combined.

+   Addition

-       Subtraction

/   Division

*   Multiplication

=	**compare data (O)**

if *Expression_1* = *Expression_2* then
statement

Tests two expressions for equality.

Expression_1, Expression_2
> The expressions being compared. They can be
> constants, variables, or the results of functions. Both
> expressions must be of the same type.

The relational operator = can be combined with the relational
operators < and > in order to test if *Expression_1* is less
than or equal to *Expression_2*, or if *Expression_1* is
greater than or equal to *Expression_2*.

<>	**compare data (O)**

if *Expression_1* <> *Expression_2* then
Statement

Tests two expressions for inequality.

Expression_1, Expression_2
> The expressions being compared. They can be
> constants, variables, or results of functions. Both
> expressions must be of the same type.

<	compare data (O)

```
if Expression_1 < Expression_2 then
Statement
```

Tests two expressions to see if one is less than the other.

Expression_1, Expression_2
> The expressions being compared. They can be constants, variables, or results of functions. Both expressions must be of the same type.

The relational operator < can be combined with the relational operator = in order to test if *Expression_1* is less than or equal to *Expression_2*.

>	compare data (O)

```
if Expression_1 > Expression_2 then
Statement
```

Tests two expressions to see if one is greater than the other.

Expression_1, Expression_2
> The expressions being compared. They can be constants, variables, or results of functions. The expressions must be of the same type.

The relational operator > can be combined with the relational operator = in order to test if *Expression_1* is greater than or equal to *Expression_2*.

Abs   absolute value (SF)

Abs (*Expression*)

Returns the absolute value of the expression. *Expression* can
be a constant, a variable, or the result of a function, and must be
either type REAL or INTEGER. The result is the same type as
the expression.

Addr   determine memory address (F)

Addr (*Expression*)

Returns the absolute address of a variable, a procedure, or a
function in memory. In 16-bit versions a 32-bit pointer to the
segment and offset is returned. In 8-bit versions, an INTEGER
value is returned as the address.

Expression

    Specifies the name of the variable, procedure, or
    function whose address you want to find. For arrays a
    specific element can be subscribed, or a specific
    component can be selected for records.

```
X:= Addr(Read_key);
X:= Addr(Table[34]);
X:= Addr(Address.Lname);
```

25

```
and                              logical operator (O)
```

Expression_1 and *Expression_2*

Evaluates bits so that the resulting bit is reset if the corresponding bit in either *Expression_1* or *Expression_2* is reset, or the resulting bit is set in both *Expression_1* and *Expression_2*.

```
and                              combine comparisons (O)
```

if *Cond_1* and *Cond_2* then *Statement*

Combines multiple comparisons. The statement is executed if *Cond_1* and *Cond_2* are both true.

Cond_1, Cond_2
> These are comparisons, using any of the relational operators =, <>, <=, >=, < or >.

```
Append                              extend a file (P)
```

Append(*File_var*)

Adds data to a file. The file pointer is placed at the end of the file. The file is available for write access only. Available only in the MS/PC-DOS version of Turbo Pascal.

File_var
> The file variable assigned to the file with **Assign**.

Arc   draw an arc (P)

Arc(*X*, *Y*, *Angle*, *Radius*, *Color*)

Draws an arc with the given angle and radius. A drawing color can be selected from the current palette in **GraphColorMode**.

X, Y   Sets the coordinates of the arc's center point. Values for *X* range from 0 to 319 or 0 to 639, depending on the graphics mode. Values for *Y* range from 0 to 199.

Angle   Specifies the angle in degrees of the arc being drawn. The arc is drawn counterclockwise if this value is negative.

Radius   Specifies the radius of the arc.

Color   The drawing color. Possible values range from 0 to 3 as indicated by the current palette in the **GraphColorMode**, or -1 for selection according to **ColorTable**. For **HiRes**, the color set with **HiResColor** is used.

Available only in the MS/PC-DOS version of Turbo Pascal. In addition, the file GRAPH.P must be included in the source code.

ArcTan   arctangent (SF)

ArcTan(*Expression*)

Returns as a REAL result the angle, in radians, of the tangent specified in *Expression*. *Expression* can be either REAL or INTEGER.

Assign   open a file (P)

Assign(*File_var,Filename*)

Opens a file for read/write access or for the use of special file
functions. The filename is assigned to the file variable. The file
variable is used to refer to the file for the rest of the program.

File_var
>   The file variable declared to be type FILE in the
>   variable declaration and is now processed:

```
type T_Record = RECORD
     Last_name: STRING[25];
   First_name: STRING[25];
   Street: STRING[25];
     City: STRING[25];
     Zip: INTEGER;
END;

var InFile: FILE of T_Record;
   Txt_file: TEXT;
   Any_file: FILE;
Assign(InFile,'TEST.DAT');
```

Filename
>   The name of the file to be opened in MS-DOS or
>   CP/M format. The specification can be a string
>   constant or a string variable.

Back   move turtle backwards (P)

Back(*Distance*)

Move the turtle backward from its current position.

Distance
> The number of pixels to move the turtle. If a
> negative number is specified, the turtle will move the
> corresponding number of steps forward.

Available only in the MS/PC-DOS version of Turbo Pascal. In
addition, the file GRAPH.P must be included in the source.

Bdos   CP/M-86 function call (P)

Bdos(*Registers*)

This procedure performs CP/M-86 function call (**Bdos**). A
record whose structure corresponds to the CPU registers must be
loaded with the necessary values and is passed as a parameter.
The result of the call is returned in the record variable or in an
area of memory reserved for this purpose.

Registers
> A variable of type RECORD containing the following
> components:

```
type Regs=RECORD CASE INTEGER OF
    1: (ax,bx,cx,dx,bp,si,di,ds,es,flags: INTEGER);
    2: (al,ah,bl,bh,cl,ch,dl,dh: BYTE);
END;

var R: Regs;
```

BIOS_function
> The number of the BIOS interrupt function to be
> executed.

Bdos/BdosHL
Bios/BiosHL   CP/M-80 calls (SP,SF)

```
Bdos(Function_num[,Parameter])
BdosHL(Function_num[,Parameter])
Bios(Function_num[,Parameter])
BiosHL(Function_num[,Parameter])
```

Bdos and **Bios** call the specified functions of the CP/M-80
Basic Disk Operating System or the Basic Input/Output System.
A parameter can be passed, that is loaded into the CPU registers
D and E.

Bdos and **Bios** return the value of the function in the A
register as an INTEGER result.

BdosHL and **BiosHL** return the value of the CP/M function
in the HL register pair.

Function_num
> The number of the function (INTEGER value) that is
> to be executed by **Bdos** or **Bios**.

Parameter
> If the function can process parameters, they are
> specified here as INTEGER values.

BlockRead   read a record from a file (P)

```
BlockRead(File_var,Dest_var,Num_recs
[,Recs_read])
```

Reads a record from an untyped file. The record length is 28
bytes. Control characters are read as normal characters. The file
must have first been opened and initialized with **Assign** and
Reset/Rewrite.

File_var
> The name of the file variable that was assigned to the
> file by **Assign**. The file type must be FILE.

Dest_var
> This is the variable that data read is placed. The size
> of the variable depends on *Num_recs* and must be
> at least 128 bytes. It must be of type array of
> BYTE, or array of CHAR.

Num_recs
> This determines how many 128-byte records are read.
> Note the destination variable must be the appropriate
> size. *Num_recs* can be any expression with an
> integer variable.

Recs_read
> *Recs_read* should be a variable of type
> INTEGER. After reading, this variable contains the
> number of records actually read.

BlockWrite   write record to a file (P)

```
BlockWrite(File_var,Dest_var,Num_recs
[,Recs_read])
```

Writes a record to an untyped file. Control characters are simply read as normal characters. The file must have first been opened and initialized with **Assign** and **Reset/Rewrite**.

File_var
> The name of the file variable that was assigned to the file by **Assign**. The file type must be FILE.

Dest_var
> The variable in which the data read are placed. The size of the variable depends on *Num_recs* and must be at least 128 bytes. It must be of type array of BYTE, or array of CHAR.

Num_recs
> The number of 128-byte records read. Note the destination variable must be the appropriate size. *Num_recs* can be any expression with an integer variable.

Recs_read
> After reading, contains the number of records actually read. *Recs_read* should be a variable of type INTEGER.

---

case
conditional statement (S)

```
case Expression of Value: Statement
else Statement end; {case}
```

Executes various statements depending on the result of an expression. Optionally, an **else** branch can be specified whose corresponding *Statement* is executed if the expression does not match any of the specified values. The **case** construction must be terminated with end.

Expression
> The value which forms the basis of the test.

Value   The value that the expression must match in order for the statement following the colon to be executed.

Statement
> The statement that is to be executed if the corresponding value matches that of *Expression*, or the statement following **else**, that is executed if none of the specified values match the expression. Multiple instructions are enclosed in a **begin...end** block.

Example:

```
repeat
  Wrong_key := False;
  Read(KBD,Ch);

  case Ch of
  '1': Enter_data;
  '2': Display_data;
  '3': Print_data;
  'E': Exit_program;
  else
    begin
      GotoXY(1,25); ClrEol;
      Write('Illegal key pressed.');
      Wrong_key := True;
    end;
  end; {case}
until not Wrong_key;
```

Chain   execute .CHN files (P)

Chain(*File_var*)

Allows Turbo Programs generated as .CHN files to be called
from a running Turbo Pascal program. .CHN files do not
contain a run-time library, but use the library of the calling
program instead. This saves disk space for larger projects.

File_var
        The file variable that was assigned to the .CHN file
        with **Assign**.

ChDir   MS-DOS directory access (P)

ChDir(*Drive:Pathname*)

Changes the specified MS-DOS directory to the current directory.

Drive   The number of the drive (INTEGER value) that you want to read the current path:

```
0= drive "A"
1= drive "B"
2= drive "C"
(etc.)
```

Pathname
             The pathname according to MS-DOS conventions.

The result of these functions should be checked with **IOresult**. **ChDir** returns an error if the specified directory is not found.

Chr   numerical→CHAR (SF)

Chr(*ASCII_code*)

Produces a character from the specified ASCII code. The result is of type CHAR and can be processed by itself or within a string function.

ASCII_code
             This can be a constant or a variable with a value between 0 and 255. The data type can be INTEGER or BYTE.

35

Circle   draw circle (P)

Circle(*X*, *Y*, *Radius*, *Color*)

Draws a circle with the given radius. A drawing color can be chosen from the current palette in **GraphColorMode**.

X, *Y*   Specifies the coordinates in the center of the circle. Values for *X* range from 0 to 319 or 0 to 639, depending on the graphics mode. Values for *Y* range from 0 to 199.

Radius   The INTEGER expression specifying the circle's radius in pixels. It is impossible to specify an axis relationship to produce ellipses instead of circles.

Color   The drawing color. Possible values are 0 to 3 as indicated by the current palette in the **GraphColorMode**, or -1 for selection according to **ColorTable**. For **HiRes**, the color set with **HiResColor** is used.

Available only in the MS/PC-DOS version of Turbo Pascal. In addition, the file GRAPH.P must be included in the source.

ClearScreen   clear turtle window (P)

ClearScreen

Clears the screen or current window. The turtle is sent to its home position (origin).

Available only in the MS/PC-DOS version of Turbo Pascal. In addition, the file GRAPH.P must be included in the source.

Close   close file (P)

Close(*File_var*)

Closes a file after read or write access or after using file functions.

File_var
          The name of the file variable assigned to the file by **Assign**.

Close must always be used after working with a file, because it is possible to lose all of the data in the file that has not been closed.

ClrEol   clear to end of line (P)

ClrEol

Clears the rest of the line on which the cursor is located starting at the current cursor position. The cursor position is unchanged.

ClrScr   clear screen (P)

ClrScr

Clears the screen and places the cursor in the upper left-hand corner.

ColorTable   change color assignment (P)

ColorTable(*Color_0, Color_1, Color_2, Color_3*)

Changes color assignments for the current palette. Here the color is set to replace the standard color. If -1 is used for the parameter color in a graphics procedure, the drawing color is set according to **ColorTable**.

Colors The standard **ColorTable** is:

        ColorTable(0,1,2,3)

Changing the table to **ColorTable(2,1,0,3)**, for example, causes *Color_2* to replace *Color_0*, *Color_1* to remain the same as before, *Color_0* to replace *Color_2*, and *Color_3* to remain unchanged.

Available only in the MS/PC-DOS version of Turbo Pascal. In addition, the file GRAPH.P must be included in the source.

Concat   concatenate strings (F)

Concat(*String,...*)

Combines two or more strings into a single string.

String,... Specifies the strings to be concatenated. Commas are
used to separate strings. String constants, string
variables, or combinations of the two can be
specified. The total string length cannot exceed 255.

The plus sign (+) can be used instead of the **Concat** function
to concatenate strings.

Copy   copy part of a string (F)

Copy(*String, Position, Num_char*)

Returns part of a string.

String The source string from which the substring is copied.
It can be either a string constant or a string variable.

Position

Specifies the position in the source string at which
the substring starts. If *Position* is outside the
length of the string, an empty string is returned.
Possible values range from 1 to 255. This value can
be a constant or a variable of type INTEGER/BYTE.

Num_char

> Specifies the number of characters returned at *Position*. Possible values range from 1 to 255. This value can be a constant or a variable of type INTEGER/BYTE.

Cos   cosine (SF)

Cos(*Expression*)

Returns as a REAL result the cosine of *Expression* given in radians. *Expression* can be either REAL or INTEGER.

CrtExit   send RESET sequence to terminal (P)

CrtExit

Sends the reset string specified during terminal installation to the terminal.

CrtInit   send INIT sequence to terminal (P)

CrtInit

Sends the initialization string defined during installation to the terminal.

Cseg   code, data and stack segment (F)

Cseg

Returns the address of the designated segment as an INTEGER
result:

        Cseg = Code segment

Available only in 16-bit versions of Turbo Pascal.

Delay   time delay (P)

Delay(*Time*)

The duration of a tone can be controlled with **Delay(*Time*)**
between **Sound** and **NoSound**.

Time   Specifies the length of the duration in milliseconds.
            Time must be given as type INTEGER.

Delay can also be used for pausing text displays, etc.
However, note that the length of the delay is dependent on the
clock frequency of the computer. The delay times vary between a
normal PC and an AT.

`Delete`   delete part of a string (P)

Delete(*String*,*Position*,*Num_char*)

Deletes a specified number of characters.

String   The name of the string variable from which the
            characters are being deleted.

Position

            Position within the *String* where the characters
            are to be deleted. If the value of *Position* is
            greater than the length of the string, no characters are
            deleted. Possible values range from 1 to 255. This
            value can be given as a constant or a variable of type
            INTEGER/BYTE.

Num_char

            Specifies the number of characters to be deleted. If
            the length of the string is exceeded as a result of the
            values specified for *Position* and *Num_char*,
            only the characters within the string are deleted.
            Possible values range from 1 to 255. This value can
            be specified as a constant or a variable of type
            INTEGER/BYTE.

`DelLine`   delete entire line (P)

DelLine

Deletes the entire line on which the cursor is located. The lines
below the deleted line are moved up automatically.

Dispose   manage pointer variables (P)

Dispose(*Pointer*)

For the management of dynamic variables (see the Turbo Pascal
Reference Manual, page 119ff), **New** reserves space for a
component of the pointer variable on the heap. After processing,
the reserved space can be released again from the heap with
Dispose.

*Pointer*The name of the pointer variable for which space is to
be reserved on the heap or whose reserved space is to
be released.

---

div   division (O)

Expression_1 div *Expression_2*

Returns as an INTEGER result the quotient of
Expression_1 divided by *Expression_2*. The
expressions must be of type REAL.

D r a w   draw a line (SP)

Draw(*From_X1,From_Y1,To_X2,To_Y2,Color*)

Draws a line from one point on the screen to another. A color
can be selected from the current palette in
GraphColorMode. A line is erased by drawing in the
background color.

From_X1,From_Y1
> Sets the starting point of the line being drawn.
> Depending on the graphics mode, values for *X1* can
> range from 0 to 319 or 0 to 639. Values for *Y1* range
> from 0 to 199.

To_X2,To_Y2
> This sets the ending point of the line being drawn.
> Depending on the graphics mode, values for *X2* can
> range from 0 to 319 or 0 to 639. Values for *Y2* range
> from 0 to 199.

Color   The drawing color. Possible values range from 0 to 3
> as indicated by the current palette in
> **GraphColorMode**, or -1 for selection
> according to **ColorTable**. For **HiRes**, the
> color set with **HiResColor** is used.

Available only in the MS/PC-DOS version of Turbo Pascal.

44

Dseg   data segment (F)

Dseg

Returns the address of the designated segment as an INTEGER result:

        Dseg = Data segment

Available only in 16-bit versions of Turbo Pascal.

EOF   test for end of file (SF)

EOF (*File_var*)

Tests whether the end of the file has been reached or not. The result is True if the file pointer points behind the last record of the file or the end-of-file marker ($1A, 26 decimal), and False if it is at some other position in the file.

File_var
        The name of the file variable assigned to the file with **Assign**.

EoLn   test for end of line (SF)

EoLn (*File_var*)

Tests for the end of the line (CR/LF, $0D/$0A) in a text file.
The result is True if the file pointer is pointing to a CR/LF and
False if it is not.

File_var
              The name of the file variable assigned to the file with
              Assign.

Erase   delete a file (P)

Erase (*File_var*)

Deletes a file opened with **Assign**.

File_var
              This is the file variable assigned to the file with
              Assign. The file variable need not have the same
              type as the file in question.

`Execute`   execute .COM files (P)

Execute(*File_var*)

Similar to **Chain**, this calls and executes one Turbo program from within another. The difference between the commands is that the called file here is a Turbo .COM file.

File_var
>   The file variable assigned to the .COM file with **Assign**.

`exit`   terminate procedure (SP)

exit

If **exit** is encountered within a procedure, the procedures are ended at this point, and execution is continued with the calling procedure. An **exit** within the main program ends the program.

`Exp`   exponent (SF)

Exp(*Expression*)

Returns as a REAL result the exponent of *Expression*. *Expression* can be of type REAL or INTEGER.

---

external   external machine language (P,F)

```
Procedure_Name; external Filename
Function_Name; external Filename
```

Includes the machine language routine stored on the disk in a
program. This routine is included in a way similar to a complete
procedure or function. In addition, an **external** file can
contain several routines. A jump table at the start of the file is
used to access the individual routines. The offset in the jump
table can be specified as follows:

```
procedure Screen; external 'SCR.BIN';
function Character: CHAR;
external Screen[3];
```

Name   The name of the procedure or function in the Pascal
program.

Filename
     The name of the file as a string constant that
contains the routine to be included.

48

FilePos   test position in file (F)

FilePos(*File_var*)

This function returns the position of the file pointer within the file as its result. The position is the number of the record to which the pointer is currently pointing. The first record in a file always has record number 0. The function **FilePos** returns an INTEGER result, and the function **LongFilePos** returns a REAL result.

File_var
> The name of the file variable assigned to the file with **Assign**.

LongFilePos is available only in the MS/PC-DOS version of Turbo Pascal. Neither of these functions can be used on text files.

FileSize   determine file size (F)

FileSize(*File_var*)

This function returns as its result the number of records stored in the file. In order to get the size in bytes, this value must be multiplied by the record length. **FileSize** returns an INTEGER result. **LongFileSize** returns a REAL result.

File_var
> The name of the file variable assigned to the file with **Assign**.

LongFileSize is available only in the MS/PC-DOS version. Neither function can be used on text files.

`FillChar`   fill variable with characters (P)

FillChar(*Variable,Number,Char*)

Fills a variable with a given character.

Variable

> The name of the variable receiving the specified character. Elements of an array or components of a record can also be specified.

Number   The number of characters to be placed in the variable. Note that **FillChar** does not check the variable to see if it is large enough to hold the specified number of characters. Use **SizeOf** to be certain of the size of the variable.

Char   The character to be received by the variable. This can be a C H A R constant or variable, or a B Y T E expression. The value must lie in the range 0 to 255.

`FillPattern`   fill area with pattern (P)

FillPattern(*X1,Y1,X2,Y2,Color*)

Fills an area with a predefined pattern in the given color. The pattern is derived from a bit mask defined with **Pattern**.

X1, Y1   The upper left corner of the area. Values for *X1* range from 0 to 319 or 0 to 639, depending on the graphics mode. Values for *Y1* range from 0 to 199.

X2, Y2   The lower right corner of the area. Values for *X2* range from 0 to 319 or 0 to 639, depending on the graphics mode. Values for *Y2* range from 0 to 199.

Color   The drawing color. Possible values range from 0 to
            3, according to the current palette in
            GraphColorMode. In **HiRes**, the color set
            by **HiResColor** is used.

Available only in the MS/PC-DOS version of Turbo Pascal. In
addition, the file GRAPH.P must be included in the source.

FillScreen   fill screen with color (P)

FillScreen(*Color*)

Fills the screen or current graphic window with the specified
color.

Color   The fill color. Possible values are 0 to 3 as indicated
            by the current palette in **GraphColorMode**, or
            -1 for selection according to **ColorTable**. In
            HiRes, the color set by **HiResColor** is used.

Available only in the MS/PC-DOS version of Turbo Pascal. In
addition, the file GRAPH.P must be included in the source.

FillShape   fill area with color (P)

FillShape (*X,Y,Fill_color,Border_color*)

Fills an area with the given fill color. This area must be made
up of a complete line, circle, polygon, etc.

X, Y   Specifies the coordinates of a point within the area to
            be filled with color. Values for *X* range from 0 to
            319 or 0 to 639, depending on the graphics mode.
            Values for *Y* range from 0 to 199.

51

Fill_color
> The color in which the area is filled. Possible values are 0 to 3, according to the current palette in **GraphColorMode**. In **HiRes**, the color set by **HiResColor** is used.

Border_color
> The border color of the area to be filled. Possible values are 0 to 3 according to the current palette in **GraphColorMode**. In **HiRes**, the color set by **HiResColor** is used.

If the shape is not entirely enclosed *Fill_color* runs onto the rest of the screen.

Available only in the MS/PC-DOS version of Turbo Pascal. In addition, the file GRAPH.P must be included in the source.

Flush	write file buffer (P)

Flush(*File_var*)

Writes the contents of the internal file buffer to the disk.

File_var
> The name of the file variable given to the file with **Assign**.

Available only in the MS/PC-DOS version.

for...do   loop processing (S)

```
for Index := Start to|downto End do
Statement
```

Executes statements repeatedly within a loop. The statements are executed until the loop index equals the end value. The index variable is incremented by one if **to** is used, and decremented by one if **downto** is used.

Index   An INTEGER variable that serves as the loop index variable.

Start   This is the initial value of the loop index.

End   This is the end value of the loop.

Statement
           The statement executed within the loop. Again, multiple statements are placed in a **begin...end** block.

The value of the index variable cannot be changed within the body of the loop. It is possible to nest multiple **for...do** loops within each other.

Forwd   move turtle forward (P)

```
Forwd(Distance)
```

Moves the turtle forward from its current position.

Distance
           The number of pixels that the turtle is to be moved. If a negative number is specified, the turtle will move the corresponding number of pixels backward.

Available only in the MS/PC-DOS version of Turbo Pascal. In
addition, the file GRAPH.P must be included in the source.

Frac   fractional portion (SF)

Frac(*Expression*)

Returns as a REAL result the fractional portion of the expression
(the numbers after the decimal point). *Expression* can be of
type REAL or INTEGER.

FreeMem   release heap memory (SP)

FreeMem(*Pointer*,*Num_bytes*)

Releases memory allocated on the heap with **GetMem**.

Pointer
> The name of the pointer variable.

Num_bytes
> An INTEGER expression whose value is the number
> of bytes to be released. The number should match the
> number of bytes allocated by **GetMem**.

GetDir   MS-DOS directory access (P)

GetDir(*Drive*,*Pathname*)

Returns the current MS-DOS directory. The result returned by
GetDir is a string in the format:

> *Drive*:*Pathname*

Drive   The number of the drive (INTEGER value) from
        which you want to read the current path:

        0= drive A
        1= drive B
        2= drive C
        (etc.)

Pathname
        The pathname according to MS-DOS conventions.

The result of these functions should be checked with
IOresult.

GetDotColor   determine point color (F)

GetDotColor(X, Y)

Returns the color of the point defined by the coordinates. In the medium-resolution graphics mode (320x200), the result is in the range 0 to 3, while in high-resolution mode, the result is either 0 or 1. If the coordinates lie outside of the screen or the current graphic window, the result is -1.

X, Y The coordinates of the point. Values for X range from 0 to 319 or 0 to 639, depending on the graphics mode. Values for Y range from 0 to 199.

Available only in the MS/PC-DOS version of Turbo Pascal. In addition, the file GRAPH.P must be included in the source.

GetMem   reserve heap memory

GetMem(*Pointer, Num_bytes*)

Reserves memory space on the heap. In contrast to **New**, *Num_bytes* are used here to determine the space to be reserved, not the size of the variable to which the pointer points.

Pointer
> The name of pointer variable.

Num_bytes
> The number of bytes to be reserved as an INTEGER value.

GetPic   store screen area (P)

GetPic(*Variable*,*X1*,*Y1*,*X2*,*Y2*)

Stores the specified screen area in a variable. From there it can
be saved to disk or returned to the screen (perhaps in a different
location) with **PutPic**.

Variable

A variable of any type to contain the data from the
screen area. This variable should be an ARRAY of
BYTE. The size of the array can be calculated
according to the following formula:

Medium-resolution (320x200):
```
Array size:= ((widthX+3) div 4) * heightY
*2 + 6
```
High-resolution (640x200):
```
Array size:= ((widthX+7) div 8) * heightY
+ 6
```

The following is stored in the first 6 bytes of the
array:

```
Bytes 1,2     graphics mode, 0001 = 640x200
Bytes 1,2     graphics mode, 0002 = 320x200
Bytes 3,4     width of the area (X)
Bytes 5,6     height of the area (Y)
```

X1, Y1   These coordinates define the upper left corner of the
area.Values for *X1* range from 0 to 319 or 0 to 639,
depending on the graphics mode. Values for *Y1* range
from 0 to 199.

X2, Y2   These coordinates define the lower right corner of the
area. Values for *X2* range from 0 to 319 or 0 to 639,
depending on the graphics mode. Values for *Y2* range
from 0 to 199.

The variable used for storing the area should be defined as larger than necessary, because **GetPic** doesn't check the variable size, and data in other variables can be overwritten.

Available only in the MS/PC-DOS version of Turbo Pascal. In addition, the file GRAPH.P must be included in the source.

---

goto   **unconditional jump (S)**

---

goto *Label*

Permits an unconditional jump to *Label*. The label must be declared in the declaration section of the applicable procedure. The jump destination must be within the same procedure that the jump occurs. If the label is declared in the declaration section of the program, a jump works only within the main program.

Label   The label name that serves as the target of the jump. The label must be followed by a colon and must be on the same line as a statement:

```
Again: Read(KBD,Ch);
if (Ch<'A') or (Ch>'C')then goto Again;
```

Labels are declared before all CONST, TYPE, or VAR declarations:

```
LABEL Again, X1, Y1;
```

GotoXY
position the cursor (P)

GotoXY *(Col, Line)*

Positions the cursor on the specified column and line.

Col   The column number at which the cursor is to be placed. Values range from 1 to 40 or 1 to 80, depending on the text mode.

Line   The line at which the cursor is to be placed. Values range from 1 to 25.

GraphBackground
set background color (SP)

GraphBackground(*Color*)

Set the background color for the medium-resolution color graphics mode (320x200). This mode must first be enabled with **GraphColorMode**.

Color   See color values under **HiresColor**.

Available only in the MS/PC-DOS version of Turbo Pascal.

GraphColorMode
320x200 color graphics (SP)

GraphColorMode

Enable the medium-resolution graphics mode with a resolution
of 320 points horizontally (X direction) and 200 points
vertically (Y direction). The display is in color. The coordinates
of the graphic procedures and functions range from 0 to 319 for
the X axis and 0 to 199 for the Y axis.

Available only in the MS/PC-DOS version of Turbo Pascal.

GraphMode
320x200 graphics (SP)

GraphMode

Enables the medium-resolution graphics mode with a resolution
of 320 points horizontally (X direction) and 200 points
vertically (Y direction). The display is in monochrome. The
coordinates of the graphic procedures and functions range from 0
to 319 for the X axis and 0 to 199 for the Y axis.

Available only in the MS/PC-DOS version of Turbo Pascal.

GraphWindow   define graphics window (P)

GraphWindow(*X1*, *Y1*, *X2*, *Y2*)

Defines a window for graphic display. The graphics are drawn only within this window. The rest of the screen is unchanged.

X1, Y1   This sets the upper left corner of the window. Depending on the graphics mode, values for *X1* can range from 0 to 319 or 0 to 639. Values for *Y1* range from 0 to 199.

X2, Y2   This sets the lower right corner of the window. Depending on the graphics mode, values for *X2* can range from 0 to 319 or 0 to 639. Values for *Y2* range from 0 to 199.

Available only in the MS/PC-DOS version of Turbo Pascal.

Halt   end program (SP)

Halt [(*Error_level*)]

Ends the program. Optionally an error level can be returned to the calling process (such as a batch file), that can then be tested. Otherwise the error level is set to zero.

Error_level
           An INTEGER value corresponding to the desired error level.

Heading   determine turtle heading (F)

Heading

Returns the current direction that the turtle is headed as an
INTEGER result . Possible values range from 0 to 359.

Available only in the MS/PC-DOS version of Turbo Pascal. In
addition, the file GRAPH.P must be included in the source.

Hi   high byte (O)

Hi(*Expression*)

Returns the high byte of the expression as an INTEGER result.
Expression must be of type INTEGER.

HideTurtle   hide turtle (P)

HideTurtle

Makes the turtle disappear (the turtle is displayed as a small
triangle on the screen or window).

Available only in the MS/PC-DOS version of Turbo Pascal. In
addition, the file GRAPH.P must be included in the source.

HighVideo   enable high intensity (P)

HighVideo

Sets the screen to display text in high intensity (bright).

HiRes   640x200 graphics (SP)

HiRes

Enable high-resolution graphics mode with a resolution of 640 points horizontally (X axis) and 200 points vertically (Y axis). Coordinates of graphic procedures and functions range from 0 to 639 for the X axis and 0 to 199 for the Y axis.

Available only in the MS/PC-DOS version of Turbo Pascal.

HiResColor   set hires drawing color (SP)

HiResColor(Color)

Set the drawing color for the high-resolution graphics mode (640x200 points). The background is always black.

Color   A number between 0 and 15 from the following table can be specified for Color.

These Turbo Pascal constants can also be used instead of numbers:

Value	Constant/color	Value	Constant/color
0	Black	8	DarkGray
1	Blue	9	LightBlue
2	Green	10	LightGreen
3	Cyan	11	LightCyan
4	Red	12	LightRed
5	Magenta	13	LightMagenta
6	Brown	14	Yellow
7	LightGray	15	White

Available only in the MS/PC-DOS version.

Home   reset turtle (P)

Home

Sends the turtle to the screen or current window's origin (home position). The heading is reset to 0 degrees.

Available only in the MS/PC-DOS version of Turbo Pascal. In addition, the file GRAPH.P must be included in the source.

---

if...then...else   conditional statement (S)

---

if *Condition* then *Statement_1* [else *Statement_2*]

Executes instructions depending on a condition. *Statement_1* is executed if the condition is fulfilled (True). Optionally, an **else** branch can be specified, in which case *Statement_2* is executed if the condition is not fulfilled (False).

Condition

The contents of a variable or the membership in a SET can be tested, or a data comparison can be made.

Statement

The statement(s) to be executed. Multiple statements are placed in a **begin...end** block.

If **else** is specified, the statement preceding the **else** cannot be terminated with a semicolon.

---

in   compare data (O)

---

if *Expression* in [SET] then *Statement*

This operator determines if *Expression* is a member of SET. The statement is executed if the expression is a member of the SET.

Expression

This is the value to be checked for possible membership in a SET:

```
var key: CHAR;
Read(KBD,key);
IF key IN ['A','B','C'] THEN ....;
```

SET   A complete or partial SET forming the basis of the
           test.

`inline`   include machine language (S)

---

inline(*Machine_code/...*)

inline generates a machine language routine within the
Turbo Pascal program. This statement can appear by itself
within a procedure or function, or it can be combined with other
statements.

Machine_code/
           The individual instruction bytes of the routine,
           separated by slashes (/):

inline($07/$1F/$5F/$00/variable/$56/$A0/$B8);

(Sample syntax only, do not enter!)

Variables are specified by inserting the name in the string within
the machine code. Note that the values of the CPU registers
must be restored after an **inline** routine has been called.
Details can be found in the Turbo Pascal Reference Manual.

Insert   insert characters into a string (P)

Insert (*Src_string*, *Dest_string*, *Position*)

Inserts a character or group of characters into the string at the specified position.

Src_string

> Specifies the character(s) to be inserted into *Dest_string*. Can be either a string constant or a string variable.

Dest_string

> Specifies the string that is to receive the characters from *Src_string*. This can also be a string constant or a string variable. The length of *Dest_string* plus the length of *Src_string* cannot exceed 255 characters.

Position

> Specifies the position in *Dest_string* at which *Src_string* is to be inserted. If *Position* lies outside of the destination string, no characters are inserted. Possible values range from 1 to 255. This value can be a constant, or an INTEGER or BYTE variable.

InsLine   insert line (P)

InsLine

Inserts a line at the current cursor position. The lines following are moved down and the last line is scrolled off the screen.

Int   integer portion (SF)

Int (*Expression*)

Returns as a REAL result the integer portion of the expression.
Expression can be of type INTEGER or REAL.

Intr   CP/M-86 function call (P)

Intr (*BIOS_function*, *Registers*)

Performs the CP/M-86 BIOS call. A record whose structure
corresponds to the CPU registers must be loaded with the
necessary values and is passed as a parameter. The result of the
call is returned in the record variable or in an area of memory
reserved for this purpose.

Registers
> A variable of type RECORD containing the following
> components:

```
type Regs=RECORD CASE INTEGER OF
    1: (ax,bx,cx,dx,bp,si,di,ds,es,flags: INTEGER);
    2: (al,ah,bl,bh,cl,ch,dl,dh: BYTE);
END;
var R: Regs;
```

BIOS_function
> The number of the BIOS interrupt function to be
> executed.

`IOresult`   trap file error (F)

X := IOresult

Returns a 0 as its result if no error occurred, or the corresponding error number, if an error occurred during a file operation. Before this option can be called, Turbo Pascal error trapping must be disabled with the {$I+}/{$I-} compiler directive:

```
Assign(D,filename);
{$I-}        {Turbo error trap off}
Reset(D);
{$I+}        {error trap back on}
IF IOresult <> 0 THEN
......error message
```

When the error trapping is turned off, you should test **IOresult** after every action. Otherwise you could get incorrect results and not know it. **IOresult** can also be used for all other run-time errors. The **I/O Error Messages** section contains a list of error messages.

`KeyPressed`   check the keyboard buffer (F)

KeyPressed

Returns True if a character is in the keyboard buffer, and False if the keyboard buffer is empty.

Length   determine the length of a string (F)

Length (*String*)

Returns the length in characters of the specified string. The result is of type INTEGER.

String   The name of the string variable whose length is to be measured.

Ln   natural logarithm (SF)

Ln (*Expression*)

Returns the natural logarithm of the expression as a REAL result. *Expression* can be of type INTEGER or REAL.

Lo   low byte (O)

Lo (*Expression*)

Returns the low byte of the expression as an INTEGER result. *Expression* must be of type INTEGER.

LongFilePos   test position in file (F)

LongFilePos(*File_var*)

Returns the position of the file pointer within the file. The position is the number of the record at which the pointer is currently pointing. The first record in a file always has record number 0. The function **FilePos** returns an INTEGER result, and the function **LongFilePos** returns a REAL result.

File_var

> The name of the file variable assigned to the file with **Assign**.

LongFilePos is available only in the MS/PC-DOS version of Turbo Pascal. It cannot be used on text files.

LongFileSize   determine file size (F)

LongFileSize(*File_var*)

Returns the number of records stored in the file. To determine the size in bytes, this value must be multiplied by the record length. **FileSize** returns an INTEGER result. **LongFileSize** returns a REAL result.

File_var

> The name of the file variable assigned to the file with **Assign**.

LongFileSize is available only in the MS/PC-DOS version. It cannot be used on text files.

LowVideo   enable low intensity (P)

LowVideo

Sets the screen to display text in low intensity (dim). All subsequent text output is displayed at normal intensity.

Mark   manipulate heap pointer (SP)

Mark(*Pointer*)

Turbo Pascal uses a *heap* for managing dynamic variables. The current value of the heap pointer can be assigned to a pointer variable with **Mark** to manage the heap. The value of a pointer variable can be assigned to the heap pointer after processing with **Release** to release the required heap space.

Pointer
> The name of a pointer variable to which the value of the heap pointer is assigned, or whose contents are assigned to the heap pointer.

Be especially careful when programming using heap management keywords—incorrect heap management can cause the computer to crash.

MaxAvail   determine free heap memory (SF)

MaxAvail

Returns the number of free 16-byte blocks (paragraphs) that are
on the heap. The result is of type INTEGER. On 8-bit versions
of Turbo Pascal, the amount of free space on the heap is returned
in bytes.

Mem   direct memory access (A)

X:=Mem[*Segment:Offset*]

Reads a value from a memory location.

Segment:Offset
        The memory address to be read. *Segment* and
        Offset are of type INTEGER. For 8-bit versions,
        only *Offset* is specified.

MemAvail   determine free memory (SF)

MemAvail

This function returns the number of free 16-byte blocks
(paragraphs) on the heap as an INTEGER result. This allows
memory to be reserved between the free blocks. On 8-bit
versions, the amount of free space on the heap is returned in
bytes.

`MemW`   direct memory access (A)

MemW[*Segment*:*Offset*] := *Value*

Writes a value to a memory location.

Segment:*Offset*
> The memory address to be written to. *Segment* and *Offset* are of type INTEGER. For 8-bit versions of Turbo Pascal, only *Offset* is specified.

Value   The BYTE value to be written to the memory location.

`MkDir`   MS-DOS directory access (P)

MkDir(*Pathname*)

Creates a directory with the specified name.

Pathname
> The pathname according to MS-DOS conventions.

The result of these functions should be checked with IOresult. MkDir returns an error if a directory with the specified pathname already exists.

---

mod   modular division (O)

Expression_1 mod *Expression_2*

Returns the integer remainder of the division of *Expression_1* by *Expression_2*. Both expressions must be of type INTEGER.

Move   move variable contents (P)

Move(*From_var,To_var,Number*)

Moves characters from one variable to another.

From_var
>The variable name from which characters are to be moved. This can also be an element of an array or a component of a record.

To_var The variable name to which the characters are to be moved. This can also be an element of an array or a component of a record.

Number The number of characters to be moved from *From_var*. Note that **Move** does not check if *To_var* can hold the specified number of characters. If *To_var* is too small, other variables can be overwritten. Use **SizeOf** to ensure variable size.

MsDos   MS-DOS function calls (P)

MsDos(*Registers*)

Performs an MS-DOS function call via interrupt 21h. A record variable whose structure corresponds to the CPU registers must be loaded with the necesary values and is passed as a parameter. The result of this purpose in the record variable or in an area of memory reserved for it.

Registers

A variable of type RECORD. The call must contain the following components:

```
type Regs=RECORD CASE INTEGER OF
1: (ax,bx,cx,dx,bp,si,di,ds,es,flags:
INTEGER);
2: (al,ah,bl,bh,cl,ch,dl,dh: BYTE);
var R: Regs;
```

New   manage pointer variables (P)

New(*Pointer*)

For the management of dynamic variables. **New** reserves space for a component of the pointer variable on the heap. After processing, the reserved space can be released again from the heap with **Dispose**.

Pointer

The name of the pointer variable for which space is to be reserved on the heap or whose reserved space is to be released.

NormVideo   enable normal video display (P)

NormVideo

Sets the screen to display text in normal intensity.

NoSound   stop sound (SP)

NoSound

Turns off tone created with **Sound**.

NoSound is available only in the MS/PC-DOS version of Turbo Pascal.

---

not   combine comparisons (O)

if not *Condition* then *Statement*

Inverts the result of a comparison.

Condition
>   This is a comparison, using any of the relational
>   operators =, <>, <=, >=, < or >.

---

not   logical operator (O)

not *Expression*

Inverts the bits of *Expression* so that a set bit is reset and a reset bit is set.

```
NoWrap                    set turtle display mode (P)
```

NoWrap

Specifies that the turle should not "wrap around" (reappear at the opposite side of the screen or window) if the turtle moves past the edge of the screen or current window.

Available only in the MS/PC-DOS version of Turbo Pascal. In addition, the file GRAPH.P must be included in the source.

```
Odd                            odd number test (SF)
```

Odd(*Expression*)

Returns True if *Expression* is an odd number, and False if the expression is an even number. *Expression* must be of type INTEGER.

```
Ofs                              determine offset (F)
```

Ofs(*Expression*)

Returns the offset of a variable, procedure, or function.

Expression
> The name of the variable, procedure, or function whose address is to be found. An array element can be indexed, or a specific component for records.

```
X:= Ofs(Read_key);
X:= Ofs(Table[34]);
X:= Ofs(Address.Lname);
```

Available only in 16-bit versions of Turbo Pascal.

o r	**combine comparisons (O)**

if *Cond_1* or *Cond_2* then *Statement*

Combines multiple comparisons. *Statement* is executed if
either *Cond_1* or *Cond_2* is fulfilled.

Cond_1, Cond_2
> These are comparisons, using any of the relational
> operators =, <>, <=, >=, < or >.

o r	**logical operator (O)**

Expression_1 or *Expression_2*

Evaluates bits so the resulting bit is set if the corresponding bits
in either *Expression_1* or *Expression_2* are set.

Ord	**CHAR→numerical (SF)**

Ord(*Character|Set_member*)

Returns an INTEGER resulting in the ordinal value of an ASCII
character or a member of a SET.

Character
> The character whose ordinal value you want to find.
> It can be a constant or a variable.

Set_member
> The member of SET whose ordinal value you want
> to find:
>
> ```
> Ord(Tuesday) — Result = 3
> Ord('A') — Result = 65
> ```

overlay   generate overlays (P)

overlay procedure|function

Creates overlays. You simply place the word **overlay** in
front of the procedures or functions in question. All consecutive
procedures or functions preceded by the word **overlay** are
assigned to an overlay module. On the diskette you will find the
modules under the name of the program with the file extensions
.000, .001, .002, etc. Space is reserved within the program
for the largest of the modules, so that all modules fit without a
problem.

During program execution, the overlay modules are loaded from
the current drive and directory. The drive and directory can be
changed with:

> ```
> OvrDrive(Drive_num)
> OvrPath(Path_name)
> ```

OvrDrive   select drive (P)

OvrDrive(Drive_num)

Designates the drive from which overlay modules are loaded.

Drive_num
> Specifies the drive number according to the following
> conventions:

```
1 = Drive A
2 = Drive B
3 = Drive C
(etc.)
```

OvrPath   select drive (P)

OvrPath(*Path_name*)

Sets the directory on the current drive from which overlay modules are loaded.

(*Path_name*)
> Specifies a path corresponding to MS-DOS conventions.

Palette   set drawing colors (P)

Palette(*Number*)

Set the color palette from which the drawing colors in medium-resolution graphics mode are selected. The graphics mode must be first enabled with **GraphColorMode**.

Number Specifies the color palette number, with the following colors available. Color 0 corresponds to the background color:

Palette	Color 1	Color 2	Color 3
0	Green	Red	Brown
1	Cyan	Magenta	LightGray
2	LightGreen	LightRed	Yellow
3	LightCyan	LightMagenta	White

Available only in the MS/PC-DOS version of Turbo Pascal.

ParamCount   MS-DOS parameter passing (F)

ParamCount

One or more parameters can be passed in MS-DOS to a program
following the program name on the command line. This feature
can also be used in Turbo Pascal programs.

ParamCount returns an INTEGER result indicating the
number of parameters following the program name.

ParamStr   MS-DOS parameter passing (F)

ParamStr(*Param_num*)

One or more parameters can be passed in MS-DOS to a program
following the program name on the command line. This feature
can also be used in Turbo Pascal programs.

ParamStr returns the individual parameters as a string.

Param_num
        The parameter number to be returned as a string.

Pattern   fill a pattern (P)

Pattern(*Pattern_var*)

Defines a bit mask used by **FillPattern**.

Pattern_var
            Defines the mask used by **FillPattern** in a
            matrix of 8x8 pixels. This variable must be of type

ARRAY [0..7] of BYTE. A set bit results in a
set point, and a cleared bit results in an unset point:

```
Pat[0]:= $AA; Pat[1]:= $55;
Pat[2]:= $AA; Pat[3]:= $55;
Pat[4]:= $AA; Pat[5]:= $55;
Pat[6]:= $AA; Pat[7]:= $55;
```

results in the following pattern:

Available only in the MS/PC-DOS version of Turbo Pascal. In
addition, the file GRAPH.P must be included in the source.

PenDown   make turtle draw (P)

PenDown

Activates the turtle's drawing pen. This mode is active until it is
disabled by **PenUp**.

Available only in the MS/PC-DOS version of Turbo Pascal. In
addition, the file GRAPH.P must be included in the source.

PenUp   stop turtle from drawing (P)

PenUp

Disables drawing pen, allowing the turtle to be moved across the screen without drawing. This mode is active until it is disabled by **PenDown**.

Available only in the MS/PC-DOS version of Turbo Pascal. In addition, the file GRAPH.P must be included in the source.

Plot   draw a point (SP)

Plot(X, Y, Color)

Draws a single point on the screen. A color can be selected from the current palette in **GraphColorMode**. A point is erased by drawing in the background color.

X, Y   The coordinates of the point being drawn. Depending on the graphics mode, values for X range from 0 to 319 or 0 to 639. Values for Y range from 0 to 199.

Color   Specifies the drawing color. Possible values range from 0 to 3 as indicated by the current palette in the **GraphColorMode**, or -1 for selection according to **ColorTable**. For **HiRes**, the color set with **HiResColor** is used.

Available only in the MS/PC-DOS version of Turbo Pascal.

Port   access to I/O ports (A)

X:= Port[*Address*]

Reads a value from a port.

Address

> The address of the port being read. This value is an
> INTEGER value.

Available only in 16-bit versions of Turbo Pascal.

PortW   access to I/O ports (A)

PortW[*Address*]:= *Value*

Writes a value to a port.

Address

> The address of the port being written to. This value
> is an INTEGER value.

Value   The BYTE expression written to the port.

Available only in 16-bit versions of Turbo Pascal.

Pos   search for a string within a string (F)

Pos(*Search_string*,*Src_string*)

Returns the position within the source string of the specified
search string. If the search string is not contained in the source
string, zero is returned.

Search_string
> Specifies the string to be located. This can be a string constant or a string variable.

Src_string
> Specifies the variable in which to search for the search string.

Pred   return predecessor (SF)

Pred(*Expression*)

Returns the predecessor of the expression. *Expression* can be of type INTEGER, BYTE, CHAR, or STRING, or from a SET.

Ptr   assign pointer value (SF)

Ptr(*Address*)

Assigns an address to a pointer variable. *Address* must be of type INTEGER.

PutPic   output area (P)

PutPic(*Variable*, *X*, *Y*)

Display an area stored by **GetPic**.

Variable
> Specifies the variable in which the area was stored, either directly by **GetPic** or read from disk.

X, Y   Defines the upper left corner of the area at which the
            data in *Variable* is displayed. Values for *X* range
            from 0 to 319 or 0 to 639, depending on the graphics
            mode. Values for *Y* range from 0 to 199.

Available only in the MS/PC-DOS version of Turbo Pascal. In
addition, the file GRAPH.P must be included in the source.

Random   generate random nunber (SF)

Random(*Expression*)

Returns a REAL random number between 0 and 1 when
Random alone is used without *Expression*. When
Random(*Expression*) is used, an INTEGER result
between 0 and *Expression* is returned.

Randomize   initialize random number (SP)

Randomize

Initializes the random number generator used with **Random**.

Read/ReadLn   keyboard input (P)

Read(*Variable*,...)
ReadLn(*Variable*,...)

Reads data from the keyboard into one or more variables.

87

Variable
> Any variable of any of the data types supported by
> Turbo Pascal. Several variables can be specified,
> separated by commas.

The maximum number of characters to be entered can be set
with the standard variable **BufLen**:

```
Write('Name of the file: ');
BufLen := 12;
ReadLn(filename);
```

The input takes place via the keyboard. The characters entered are
displayed on the screen. If the logical device KBD is specified,
the characters are not displayed as they are typed.

```
Read(KBD,Ch);
```

Read/ReadLn   file reading (P)

Read(*File_var,Dest_var*)
ReadLn(*File_var,Dest_var*)

Reads data from a file opened with **Assign** and initialized
with Reset. A character or line is read from a text file, or a
record from any other file.

File_var
> The name of the file variable assigned to the file with
> **Assign**.

Dest_var
> The variable in which the data read is assigned. If no
> destination variable is given for a text file, the next
> line is skipped.

88

Release   manipulate heap pointer (SP)

Release(*Pointer*)

Turbo Pascal uses a *heap* for managing dynamic variables. The current value of the heap pointer can be assigned to a pointer variable with **Mark** to manage the heap. The value of a pointer variable can be assigned to the heap pointer after processing with **Release** to release the required heap space.

Pointer
> The name of a pointer variable to which the value of the heap pointer is assigned, or whose contents are assigned to the heap pointer.

Release and the **Dispose** procedure cannot be used together. **Release** can only free memory in the heap that lies above the value of the pointer variable, while **Dispose** releases the space actually used in the heap.

Rename   change the name of the file (P)

Rename(*File_var*, *New_name*)

Change the name of an existing file. The file must first have been opened with **Assign**.

File_var
> The name of the file variable assigned to the file with **Assign**.

New_name
> The string constant or variable that contains the new name of the file.

repeat...until   loop processing (S)

repeat *Statements* until *Condition*

Repeats execution of *Statements* until *Condition* is True.
The statements are executed <u>before</u> *Condition* is checked.

Statement
          The statement to be executed. Multiple statements
          can be combined into a **begin...end** block.

Condition
          Here variable contents or the membership of a SET
          can be checked, or a data comparison can be made.

Reset   initialize file (P)

Reset(*File_var*)

After **Assign**, the file must be initialized. **Reset** places the
file pointer at the first record in the file.

File_var
          The name of the file variable assigned to the file with
          Assign.

For a text file, only read operations can be carried out after
Reset. If a record is to be written, the file must be initialized
with **Append**. The records are then appended to the end of the
file. Both read and write accesses can be made to files of other
types.

`Rewrite`   overwrite file (P)

Rewrite(*File_var*)

When an existing file is to be overwritten, it must be initialized
with **Rewrite**. Read accesses are no longer than possible.

File_var
>   The name of the file variable assigned to the file with
>   **Assign**.

`RmDir`   MS-DOS directory access (P)

RmDir(*Pathname*)

Access to the directory structure of MS-DOS. **RmDir** deletes
the specified directory

The result should be checked with **IOresult**. **RmDir**
returns an error if there are still files or subdirectories in the
directory to be deleted.

`Round`   round off number (SF)

Round(*Expression*)

Rounds off the REAL *Expression*. The result is of type
INTEGER.

| **Seek** | position file pointer (P) |

Seek(*File_var*, *Rec_num*)

Positions the file pointer to a specific record within the file. The numbering of records always starts with 0.

File_var
> The variable name assigned to the file with **Assign**.

Rec_num
> The contents of the file pointer is replaced by the value of this expression.

Seek cannot be used on text files.

| **SeekEof** | seek end of file (SF) |

SeekEof(*File_var*)

Similar to **EOF**. The difference from **EOF** is that spaces ($20, 32 decimal), tabs ($09, 9 decimal), and end-of-line markers (CR/LF, $0D/$0A, 13 decimal/10 decimal) are skipped before the end of file is checked. The result is True if the file pointer points past the end of the file or to the end-of-file marker ($1A, 26 decimal), and False if it points somewhere else.

File_var
> The name of the file variable assigned to the file with **Assign**.

`SeekEoln`   find end of line (SF)

SeekEoln(*File_var*)

Similar to **EoLn**. The difference is that if the file pointer is on a space (\$20, 32 decimal), or a tab character (\$09, 9 decimal), it is moved beyond the space or tab and the next character is tested. The result is True if the file pointer then points to a CR/LF, and False if it is pointing to some other character.

File_var
> The name of the file variable assigned to the file with **Assign**.

`Seg`   determine segment (F)

Seg(*Expression*)

Returns the segment of a variable, procedure, or function in memory.

Expression
> The name of the variable, procedure or function whose segment you want found. A specific element or specific component selected for records can be subscribed:

```
X:= Seg(Read_key);
X:= Seg(Table[34]);
X:= Seg(Address.Lname);
```

Available only in 16-bit versions of Turbo Pascal.

93

SetHeading   set turtle heading (P)

SetHeading(*Angle*)

Sets the absolute direction that the turtle will travel if it is
moved forward.

Angle   The desired angle for the heading in degrees. Possible
           values range from 0 to 359.

           The following Turbo Pascal constants can also be
           used instead of the numbers:

Constant	Angle
North	0 degrees (up)
East	90 degrees (right)
South	180 degrees (down)
West	270 degrees (left)

Available only in the MS/PC-DOS version of Turbo Pascal. In
addition, the file GRAPH.P must be included in the source.

SetPenColor   set turtle drawing color (P)

SetPenColor(*Color*)

Sets the drawing color for turtlegraphics.

Color   The drawing color. Possible values range from 0 to 3
           according   to   the   current   palette   in
           GraphColorMode, or -1 for the color selection
           by **ColorTable**. In **HiRes** the color set by
           HiResColor is used.

Available only in the MS/PC-DOS version of Turbo Pascal. In addition, the file GRAPH.P must be included in the source.

SetPosition   position turtle (P)

SetPosition(X, Y)

Moves the turtle to the specified screen or window coordinates.

X, Y   The coordinates of the turtle's destination.

Available only in the MS/PC-DOS version of Turbo Pascal. In addition, the file GRAPH.P must be included in the source.

---

shl   shift left (O)

Expression shl Num_bits

Logically shifts the bits of Expression to the left by Num_bits. The rightmost Num_bits of Expression are filled with zero-bits. Expression must be of type INTEGER.

ShowTurtle   display turtle (P)

ShowTurtle

Makes the turtle visible if it was invisible before.

Available only in the MS/PC-DOS version of Turbo Pascal. In addition, the file GRAPH.P must be included in the source.

```
shr                                    shift right (O)
```

Expression shr *Num_bits*

Logically shifts the bits of *Expression* to the left by *Num_bits*. The rightmost *Num_bits* of *Expression* are filled with zero-bits. *Expression* must be of type INTEGER.

```
Sin                                         sine (SF)
```

Sin(*Expression*)

Returns the sine of the angle specified in radians. *Expression* can be of type INTEGER or REAL; the result is of type REAL.

```
SizeOf                              variable size (SF)
```

SizeOf(*Variable*)

Returns as an INTEGER result the space in bytes occupied by *Variable*.

```
Sound                                  play tone (SP)
```

Sound(*Frequency*)

Plays a note of the specified frequency through the monitor loudspeaker. This note will play indefinitely until stopped by **NoSound**, or it can be held for the length specified by **Delay**.

96

Frequency

Specifies the frequency of the note in Hertz. *Frequency* is an expression of type INTEGER.

Sound is available only in the MS/PC-DOS version of Turbo Pascal.

Sqr   square (SF)

Sqr (*Expression*)

Returns the square of the expression. *Expression* can be of type INTEGER or REAL. The result is of the same type as the expression.

Sqrt   square root (SF)

Sqrt (*Expression*)

Returns as a REAL result the square root of the expression. *Expression* can be of type INTEGER or REAL.

Sseg   stack segment (F)

Sseg

Returns the address of the designated segment as an INTEGER result:

        Sseg = Stack segment

Available only in 16-bit versions of Turbo Pascal.

Str   numerical→string (P)

Str(*Expression:Format,String*)

Converts a numerical expression into a string. Simple formatting can be applied.

Expression
> Specifies the constant or variable being converted to a string. *Expression* can be of type BYTE, INTEGER, or REAL.

Format   This formats the destination string. For INTEGER variables, this specifies the number of digits. For example:

```
Str(file_size:8,Dummy);
```

> For REAL values you can define the number of digits before and after the decimal point as follows:

```
Str(Salary:5:2,Dummy);
```

> The formatting is right-justified in the destination string.

String   The name of the string variable in which the result is placed.

Succ   successor (SF)

Succ(*Expression*)

Returns the successor of the expression. *Expression* can be of type INTEGER, BYTE, CHAR, or STRING, or from a SET.

`Swap`   high/low byte exchange (SF)

`Swap(Expression)`

Exchanges the low and high bytes of the INTEGER expression
and returns an INTEGER result.

`TextBackground` text background color (P)

`TextBackground(Color)`

Sets the text background color for display on the screen.

`Color`   See `TextColor` for details on this parameter.

`TextColor`   select text color (P)

`TextColor(Color)`

Sets the text color for display on the screen.

`Color`   A value between 0 - 15 from the table on the next
           page can be entered for `Color`.

These Turbo Pascal constants can also be used in place of the numbers:

Value	Constant/color	Value	Constant/color
0	Black	9	LightBlue
1	Blue	10	LightGreen
2	Green	11	LightCyan
3	Cyan	12	LightRed
4	Red	13	LightMagenta
5	Magenta	14	Yellow
6	Brown	15	White
7	LightGray	16	Blink
8	DarkGray		

The characters will flash on and off by adding 16 to the color number (e.g., 17 produces flashing blue characters) or adding Blink to the text color (for example, TextColor(Blue + Blink)).

TextMode   select text mode (P)

TextMode(Mode)

Changes the screen from graphics mode to text mode. In addition, the number of characters per screen line is specified.

Mode   The following values can be given for Mode:

```
0/BW40  = monochrome 40 characters/line
1/BW80  = monochrome 80 characters/line
2/C40   = color 40 characters/line
3/C80   = color 80 characters/line
```

The specifications BW40, BW80, C40, and C80 are Turbo Pascal constants and can be used in place of the numbers 0, 1, 2, and 3 respectively.

`Trunc`   return integer (SF)

Trunc(*Expression*)

Returns as an INTEGER result the next integer larger than the
expression if less than zero, and the next smaller integer if the
expression is larger than zero.

`Truncate`   truncate file (P)

Truncate(*File_var*)

Truncates a file. All records after the file pointer are lost.

File_var
> The name of the file variable assigned to the file with
> **Assign**.

Available only in the MS/PC-DOS version.

`TurnLeft`   set turtle direction (P)

TurnLeft(*Angle*)

Rotates the turtle to the left by the given angle relative to its
current position. For example, if the heading of the turtle is 45
degrees and **TurnLeft(37)** is given, the heading is then 8
degrees. **SetHeading(37)** would set the heading to 37
degrees.

Angle   The number of degrees to rotate the turtle. A positive
value turns the turtle counterclockwise (left), while a
negative value turns it clockwise (right).

101

Available only in the MS/PC-DOS version of Turbo Pascal. In addition, the file GRAPH.P must be included in the source.

`TurnRight`   set turtle direction (P)

TurnRight(*Angle*)

Rotates the turtle to the right by the given angle relative to its current position (cf. **SetHeading**). For example, if the heading of the turtle is 45 degrees and you specify **TurnRight(37)**, the heading is then 82 degrees. **SetHeading(37)** would set the heading to 37 degrees.

Angle   The number of degrees the turtle is to be rotated. A positive value turns the turtle clockwise (right). A negative value turns it counterclockwise (left).

Available only in the MS/PC-DOS version of Turbo Pascal. In addition, the file GRAPH.P must be included in the source.

`TurtleDelay`   set turtle delay (P)

TurtleDelay(*Time*)

Sets a delay between turtle movements. Normally the turtle moves immediately after a movement command.

Time   Specifies the time delay in milliseconds before the movement is executed.

Note: The delay is dependent on the clock frequency of the computer. Delay times can vary between PC and AT models.

Available only in the MS/PC-DOS version of Turbo Pascal. In addition, the file GRAPH.P must be included in the source.

TurtleThere   turtle status (F)

TurtleThere

Returns True if the turtle is visible on the screen or window, and
False if it has been hidden with **HideTurtle**.

Available only in the MS/PC-DOS version of Turbo Pascal. In
addition, the file GRAPH.P must be included in the source.

TurtleWindow   define turtle window (P)

TurtleWindow(*Origin_X, Origin_Y, Width_X,
Height_Y*)

Defines a window for turtlegraphics. In contrast to normal
graphics, the coordinates are specified differently; the origin (0,0)
is at the center of the screen. From there the X coordinates to the
left of the origin range from -159 or -319 up to 0, the X
coordinates to the right of the origin range up to 160 or 320. Y
coordinates above the origin go through 100. The Y coordinates
below the origin extend to -99.

Origin_X, Origin_Y
> Set the origin of the turtlewindow. The specifications
> refer to the standard graphic screen.

Width_X, Height_Y
> Set the width and height of the turtlewindow in
> pixels.

Available only in the MS/PC-DOS version of Turbo Pascal. In
addition, the file GRAPH.P must be included in the source.

103

UpCase   convert lower-case into upper-case (F)

`UpCase(Character)`

Returns the upper-case equivalent of the specified character. If `Character` is not a letter, it is unchanged.

`Character`
> Specifies the constant or variable containing the character to be converted. This must be of type BYTE, CHAR, or STRING.

UpCase can be used within a **for...do** loop to convert an entire string to upper case:

```
FOR I:= 1 to Length(String) DO
String[I]:=UpCase(String[I]);
```

Val   string→numerical (P)

`Val(String,Num_var,Error)`

Converts a string containing numbers to a numerical variable. An error flag is set if the string contains non-numerical characters.

`String`   The name of the string to be converted into a numerical variable. The string can contain only the digits 0 through 9, E+ or E− for the exponent, and the decimal point. All other characters set the error flag.

`Num_var`
> The numerical variable name in which the result is placed. The data type of the numerical variable determines the type of the result.

104

Error   The name of an INTEGER variable is placed here.
            This variable contains a zero if the conversion was
            performed correctly. Otherwise it contains the
            position within the string that the conversion
            stopped because an illegal character was discovered.

`WhereX/WhereY`   find cursor position (F)

WhereX
WhereY

Return the current column (**WhereX**) and line (**WhereY**)
where the cursor is located. Both functions return values of type
INTEGER.

`while...do`   loop processing (S)

---

while *Condition* do *Statement*

Executes statements repeatedly as long as the condition is True.
The condition is checked, then the statement is executed if True.

Condition
            Here variable contents or the membership of a SET
            can be checked, or a data comparison can be made.

Statement
            The statement to be executed. Multiple statements
            can be combined into a **begin...end** block.

It is possible to nest multiple **while...do** loops.

Window   define text window (P)

Window(*Col_1,Line_1,Col_2,Line_2*)

Sets a window for text output.

Col_1,Line_1
> The column and line of the upper left corner of the window.

Col_2,Line_2
> The column and line of the lower right corner of the window.

Values for the *Col* parameters range from 1 to 25. Values for the *Line* parameters range from 1 to 40, or 1 to 80.

All subsequent procedures and functions affect the newly defined window only. For example, **ClrScr** will clear only the area of the new window, not the entire screen.

---

with...do   record simplification (S)

with *Record* do *Statement*

Simplifies working with records in the program. For example, normal record assignment works as follows:

```
Address.Lname := 'Smith';
Address.Fname := 'John';
Address.Street := '101 Main St.';
```

Using **with...do**, an assignment for handling the same data looks like this:

```
with Address do
  begin
    Lname := 'Smith';
    Fname := 'John';
    Street := '101 Main St.';
  end; {with Address do}
```

Record The name of the record variable that the following statement refers.

Statement

The statement or block to be executed. The statement(s) do not all need to refer to the record, but accomplish other tasks. Multiple statements are placed in a **begin...end** block.

Wrap	set turtle display mode (P)

Wrap

Specifies that the turle should "wrap around" (reappear at the opposite side of the screen or window) if the turtle moves past the edge of the screen or current window. Normally, if the turtle moves past the edge of the screen or current window, it stays out of sight (**NoWrap**).

Available only in the MS/PC-DOS version of Turbo Pascal. In addition, the file GRAPH.P must be included in the source.

Write/WriteLn   output to the screen (P)

```
Write([LST]Expression[:before_dec
[:after_dec]])
Writeln([LST]Expression[:before_dec
[:after_dec]])
```

Outputs data of any type to the screen. A certain degree of formatting can be specified. **WriteLn** causes a linefeed to be added after the output, while **Write** does not.

Expression
>   Specifies variables, constants, or results of calculations or functions. Several expressions can be combined, separated by commas.

before_dec
>   Allows simple formatting of integer values or strings. *Before_dec* specifies the length of the output field and the output is right-justified. For real values, this determines the number of places that are displayed before the decimal point.

after_dec
>   Specifies the number of places after the decimal point for real numbers. The output takes place in a field *before_dec* + *after_dec* in length, plus one place for the decimal point.

The output from **Write** and **WriteLn** goes to the screen by default. Declaring the logical device L S T preceding *Expression* sends the output to a printer:

```
Writeln(LST,'This will go to the printer');
```

Write/WriteLn   write data to a file (P)

```
Write(File_var,Data_var)
WriteLn(File_var,Data_var)
```

Writes data to a file opened with **Assign** and initialized with
Rewrite or **Reset**.

File_var
> The name of the file variable assigned to the file with
> **Assign**.

Data_var
> The variable that contains the data to be written. The
> variable type must correspond to the file type.

WriteLn can only be used with text files. If no data variable
is specified for a text file, a blank line (CR/LF, $0D/$0A, 13
decimal/10 decimal) is written.

Xcor   determine turtle X coordinate (F)

```
Xcor
```

Return as an INTEGER result the current X coordinate of the
turtle position on the screen or current window.

Available only in the MS/PC-DOS version of Turbo Pascal. In
addition, the file GRAPH.P must be included in the source.

---

xor   logical operator (O)

Expression_1 xor *Expression_2*

Evaluates bits so that the resulting bit is reset of the
corresponding bits in both *Expression_1* to
Expression_2 are equal. Otherwise, the resulting bit is set.

Ycor   determine turtle Y coordinate (F)

Ycor

Returns as an INTEGER result the current Y coordinate of the
turtle position on the screen or current window.

Available only in the MS/PC-DOS version of Turbo Pascal. In
addition, the file GRAPH.P must be included in the source.

I/O Error Messages

The error numbers are output in hexadecimal.

Error message	Error number
File does not exist.	01
File not open for input.	02
File not open for output.	03
File not open.	04
Error in numeric format.	10
Operation not allowed on a logical device.	20
Not allowed in direct mode.	21
Assign to std files not allowed.	22
Record length mismatch.	90
Seek beyond end-of-file.	91
Unexpected end-of-file.	99
Disk write error.	F0
Directory is full.	F1
File size overflow.	F2
Too many open files.	F3
File disappeared.	FF

QuickIndex

This index lists all of Turbo Pascal's commands in alphabetical order, for quick reference:

Subject Index

*This index lists Turbo Pascal's command set by general subject,
the keyword descriptions grouped within the subject heading, and
the keywords themselves to the right of the descriptions:*

Branching

Compiler Directives

Constants, Types and Variables

Data Comparison

Data Conversion

File Management

Heap and Dynamic Variables

Installation

Keyboard Input

Machine language

Mathematics

Memory Access and Ports

MS-DOS|CP/M commands

Printer Output

Screen Management

Screen Output

Standard Graphics

Index

Quick Program Reference Guides

The Program Reference Guide series from Abacus gives busy people like you the essential PC information you need—right now.

These lightweight, convenient books are designed specifically to give you lightning-fast access to the most popular PC software. It's *instant information at your fingertips.*

Concise

- PRG's easily fit in your coat pocket or purse—and take up a lot less space on your desk than all those user manuals, books & binders.

Portable

- Have a PC at home, as well as the office? Slip a PRG (or two, or three...) into your briefcase. Leave those heavy reference books up on the shelf.

Light-weight

- Have a laptop PC? Slip a couple of PRG's into the computer's carrying case. But don't try this with your user's manuals.

Durable

- PRG's are hardcover books that stand up to heavy daily use. And PRG's are priced right at $12.95 each.

You'll find our little Program Reference Guides are indispensible. That's why we're writing them for all of the major PC application software packages.

Try one. You'll be back for more.

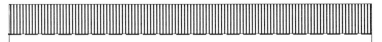

MS-DOS
Describes all of the DOS commands through version 3.2; lists parameters, options, and syntax. Complete sections on batch files, configuration, more.

Microsoft
Word
Concise, tightly organized guide to Word's menus, commands, command fields, options, shortcuts, and the mouse. Complete sections on advanced features—form letters, indexing, and more.

Microsoft
GW-BASIC
Complete description of the BASIC commands, syntax and parameters at a glance.

dBASE III/III+
Complete guide listing commands with syntax, options, and description of their use.

Lotus
1 - 2 - 3
Quick access to 1-2-3 commands, options, more. Essential reference for any 1-2-3 user.

Turbo Pascal
Handy reference of Turbo's reserved words, parameters, syntax and keywords.

Other titles
available soon:

Multiplan

Wordstar

Word Perfect

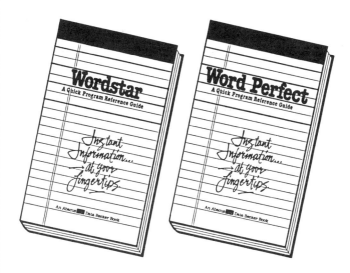

and more coming

Order Info
for Program Reference Guides

- Each Program Reference Guide is available from more than 2000 dealers and bookstores in the U.S. and Canada. To find out the dealer location nearest to you, call:

(616) 241-5510
8:30 am-8:00 pm Eastern Standard Time

- If they don't stock the PRG you're looking for, order from us directly by phone. We accept Mastercard, Visa and American Express.

For *extra-fast* 24-hour shipment service,
order by phone with your credit card

Abacus
P.O. Box 7219
Grand Rapids, MI 49510

Phone: (616) 241-5510   Fax: (616) 241-5021   Telex: 709-101

Order Blank

Name: _____

Address: _____

City: _____ State: _____ Zip: _____

Phone: _____ / _____ Country: _____

Qty	Title	Price
		$12.95
		$12.95
		$12.95
		$12.95
		$12.95
		$12.95
	Mich. residents add 4% sales tax	
	Shipping/Handling charge (Foreign Orders $4.00 per item)	$2.00
	Check/Money order TOTAL enclosed	

Credit Card#

| | | | | | | | | | | | | | | | | | | |

Expiration date   *Cardholder Signature*

| | | |

_____

Send your completed order blank to:

Abacus
P.O. Box 7219
Grand Rapids, MI 49510

Your order will be shipped within 24 hours our our receiving it.
**For extra-fast 24-hour shipment service, order by phone with
your credit card—call (616) 241-5510.**